Network Marketing Survival

Jim Stephens

Terms and Conditions

LEGAL NOTICE

Table Of Contents

Introduction

Network marketing is not the same old routine it was in the Baby Boomers' generation. Several things have changed. Things like door-to-door calls, cold calling, etc. are just passé. Today, network marketing has gone online in a very large way.

Here, in this eBook, we shall see how people have taken network marketing ahead and what you can do to realize its full potential.

Chapter 1:

An Introduction

Summary

Network marketing isn't what it once was. Times have changed and so has this concept. In this chapter we begin to understand how network marketing is placed in today's times.

An Introduction

Whatever may have changed with the network marketing world, one thing remains quite constant. This realm is just as competitive as it ever was. And that's the reason you need to employ improved strategies if you have to run ahead in the race. People have become wise to all the new tricks and it is time we brought something new into our methods.

Network marketing still works with the jungle mentality. The lions eat the hares. That's one thing that has not changed.

Network marketing has come a long, long way from the fifties when it was first introduced as a business model. However, there are some things that haven't yet changed much.

→ It is still very important to give good value to the people in your team.
→ It is still observed that people at the top (uplines) help the people at the bottom (downlines). Sidelines help each other as well.
→ Management is still of prime essence.
→ It is extremely crucial to have your own standing and reputation if you are to make any kind of headway into this world.

Of course, these points are of timeless importance. The basic essence of network marketing still follows through in the 21st century, but the methods in which these are planned have undergone a sea change. Methods of finding opportunities, methods of prospecting people and methods of keeping one step ahead of the competition have decidedly changed.

Here you shall learn how these new tendencies can be employed to make the best of your network marketing endeavors. You can learn what methods work and what won't.

At the same time, it needs to spelled out, right here at the outset, that just reading this eBook is not going to make you the next network marketing guru. You have to employ the methods described herein and take advantages of our suggestions if you have to make the business work for you.

Chapter 2:

Network Marketing in the 21st Century

Summary

So how different has network marketing become really?

Network Marketing in the 21st Century

You have to know some important differences first.

Sales Vs Marketing

Prospects have become warier than they ever were. There are so many opportunities out there that it is difficult for them to decide what they must take, if at all. Even if someone is contemplating on a network marketing business, you couldn't always hope to sway them toward your side because there are so many options opened out to them.

However, network marketing still remains lucrative and that is one big draw for you to bring people toward your business. The results that can be expected can be so huge in monetary terms that they could put most companies to shame.

The emphasis of 'marketing' in 'network marketing' is still quite profound. Despite whatever you might have heard about networking being the most important thing here, you must know that you are, after all, 'marketing'. This is an important thing for you to consider. In fact, when you are getting your prospects, make sure that you get people who know how to market. Networking is fine enough, but what use is it if you can get your octogenarian grandmother into your network, who cannot market anything for you?

The days of pumping network with people who cannot market – read family and friends – should be over by now. Today's network marketing businesses know that it is extremely important to have people in the team who can bring about the all important sales.

Though this premise is slightly different, network marketing is most assuredly a sales concept. You have to sell things for money, not just share them.

In the 21st century, the difference between sharing and selling has become much more profound, especially over the Internet. When you recommend something without any financial gains, like if you tell someone there's a really great movie in town that they must catch, you aren't selling. Selling is what is important in network marketing – you do this with monetary gains involved for yourself.

Chapter 3:

The Google Revolution

Summary

Googling might well become an Oxford entry. It is not a matter of 'will it', it is a matter of 'when'.

The Google Revolution

As in everything else, the Google Revolution has swept the network marketing world as well. A very small indication can be obtained by simply going to Google and typing in 'network marketing'. With 123,000,000 results, there's no questioning how popular this search term is, and Google won't ever be behind to latch on to something that is so much in demand.

But, why is Google important to you? It is so simply because now Google has overtaken all other search engines in popularity. It has become almost an Internet default to search something on Google. If you don't know something or want to find out something, no one any longer says, "I will search on the Internet." Instead, they say, "I will Google it."

Hence, if you rank on Google, if you get those highly coveted first page rankings, you have it made. Now, Google SEO is a whole new concept in itself. But remember these few things:–

1. Google ranks websites on the basis of their content. So, content remains king. However, this content is useless unless it has the right kind of content involved in it.
2. Along with that, Google simply loves it if you update your content regularly. That is why blogs are tops.
3. Inbound links are just something else when you are dealing with Google. Get as many links live on the Internet – through articles, blogs, forum posts, social networking site comments, etc. The more the number of people visiting your site, the better will be the rank of the site.

Today, working with Google has become like a circle. You first promote yourself on Google, get the initial trickle of visitors, and when Google sees that people are visiting your website, they will rank your site better which will help attract more visitors. It is actually simple to get the initial rank on Google if you follow all Google-friendly methods. Get in the loop as fast as you can.

At the same time, don't forget Google's value in research. You could use this tool significantly in finding out what your competitors are really up to and you could enhance your strategies likewise.

Chapter 4:

Finding the Right Opportunity

Summary

Whatever hopes you might have, whatever you must have thought about the whole thing, however much confident you might be about yourself, all that could be squashed with just one wrong initial move.

Finding the Right Opportunity

Ask yourself this question several times over before getting into the network marketing venture you will eventually choose –
"Why am I getting into network marketing?"

Unless and until that still small voice inside you says that you are getting into it for making money, you are not going to get a good start.

Think about it. Your network marketing venture is special because you are in this for the pure and sole reason for making money. Make this your utmost intention. In the 21st century, with the high level of competitiveness all around, this point has become more poignant than ever.

Here is the mindset that you need to inculcate so that you make sure you are landing with the right opportunity for yourself.

You Are a Businessperson

Whatever name your company might use for you – distributor, sponsor, MLM leader – what you really need to know is that you are a businessperson, an entrepreneur. This might be a small business for now, but it has the potential to go as much ahead as you can dream.

So, what's the position of the network marketing company you are collaborating with? No, it's not your boss as you might think. It is your business partner.

This is what you need to keep in mind. You are partnering with this company to make your profits. The company needs you more than you need it. At least in the initial stages.

Get the Right Company

In order to ensure that you get the right network marketing company to partner with, these are the important things that you need to check out:-
  → What is their reputation? Do they have a great track record?

→ Are they permanent? It is a very good idea to check their history. If they are a long-standing company, you could almost bank on it.

→ Are they dynamic? You need a company that doesn't mind planning out and implementing new ideas. Remember that in the 21st century, things are moving fast – too fast actually – and companies that remain stuck in the mud won't do much.

→ Check their vision out. What do they plan to achieve in the next year? In the next five years? Can you see yourself growing with the company?

→ What is their product? A lot of your judgment should depend on what product they are selling. Indeed, if the product is good and in demand, you have a better scope of evolving with the company.

Chapter 5:

Finding the Right Team

Summary

Most times, you are your own enemy. You get in the way of making yourself rich. You need to vanquish yourself to an extent to get those riches.

Finding the Right Team

When you join in, the team that concerns you is your upline. These are the people who are already present. It is vital that your upline is supportive of you. They have to guide you through and then stay like moral supports for you. A good upline is decidedly important in helping you grow your own activities.

One of the things that you need to check out in your upline is whether they are supportive of new ideas. This can actually be checked by you at the initial stages itself when they are prospecting you. First, understand what they say and then tell them of a suggestion or an idea that you have. Here, you will understand how dynamic they are. Once you have their answer, you will know whether these will be good people on your team or not.

Besides that, here are some things that you have to feel out before you join a network marketing team.

Support

It is ultra-vital that their support should be speedy. If it isn't, you might just lose out on your learning process and not make a headway at all. Support is not important just within your upline; it is also extremely important within your downline. If your downline doesn't provide good support, it could be a deterrent in bringing new people into the team. It is only when your team as a whole can provide capable support will other people have no qualms about joining it.

Being Extroverted

As far as possible, avoid close-knit groups. Such people have a heightened impression about themselves but it could be very regressive being with them. The reason for that is such groups get cloistered and don't make progress. They remain cocooned within their networks, which is again the whole concept of network marketing. If you are into network marketing, it is vital that you reach out to other people.

Chapter 6:

Understanding Compensation Plans

Summary

The real money is in understanding the compensation plans.

Understanding Compensation Plans

One of the most important things for you to do before going ahead with a particular network marketing venture is to find out what kind of compensation plan they have. There are several compensation plans actually. A few of these plans are quite simple, but then there are complicated plans too, which might take some understanding on your part.

It is absolutely vital that you understand your compensation plan in its entirety because this is what most people will use when they have to decide whether they want to join your downline or not. You will have to explain your compensation plan to a lot of people. They will ask you a lot of questions. If you are not able to answer them, they won't be so confident about joining your venture.

At the same time, you have to understand the compensation plan for yourself. If you don't, you might not realize what you are missing out on. You might be missing just small sums but these could amount to something huge when you think about the long run.

Single and Multilevel Compensation Plans

These are the first two that you have to learn about.

Single Compensation Plans – Most of the businesses of the world work on this premise. You buy something from a seller and you pay the seller the price for it. Now, the seller could be an affiliate or a salesperson. So the price you are actually paying the seller for the product is a commission. In this model, there is just one level – the seller. Hence, this is a single compensation plan. This model does not benefit the seller much; it is the manufacturer who keeps the bulk of the payment that you make.

Multilevel Compensation Plans – Here, you find several tiers of marketers, each one trying to sell a product. Here, the company that manufactures the item will eventually get the price of the item, but there will be a lot of reduction in what the consumer actually pays. The reason for that is there will be a lot of commissions paid out to the people in the network that sold the item. Every company has their own rules regarding how many upline members must earn their commissions on a particular sale.

Now, these are the points you need to bear in mind when you are looking at the compensation plans of your network marketing opportunity.

1. Shop around. Some opportunities pay more than the others. Don't take up the first opportunity that comes your way.
2. Multilevel plans are better than single compensation plans because the commissions can have a better snowballing effect from the sponsors.
3. There are two types of scenarios here – Some plans pay more commission to people immediately in their downline and the members in the downline's downline will get lesser commission. The second scenario is when some plans pay more to people who build their networks, in which the entire network makes a profit. Make sure you see which scenario applies to your network marketing opportunity.

Besides that, there are several kinds of network marketing plans within the multilevel framework.

Unilevel Plans

These have the highest commission for the first level and the commission goes on reducing drastically for every subsequent down level. However, the plan has no restriction on how many people earn commissions within the first level. This plan can be best described by – *unlimited width, limited depth.*

Stairstep Plans

There is a ranking system here, and the level that gets the best rank gets the best commissions. The ranking applies to only the members in the first level. The other members also get their commissions, but they are significantly lower.

Binary Plans

These plans are quite simple and uncomplicated. Each member is supposed to have just two other members.

Besides there, there is a complicated network marketing compensation plan known as the Australian two-up which some businesses are using nowadays.

Chapter 7:

Methods of Prospecting

Summary

Enticing people to join your team – how to do it?

Methods of Prospecting

Methods of prospecting have definitely undergone a sea change in recent times. The following are some of the trends that have passed out.

Cold Calling

With the large number of highly effective methods available currently, no one cold calls anymore. There's no reason why someone should call up a total stranger, when it is very much possible to get targeted people as prospects. At the same time, marketers themselves are understanding that they don't like getting calls about sales methods and people have developed a kind of total apathy to anything that is being peddled through the phone, even if the company has quite a reputation otherwise.

Invitations

The same applies to invitations to workshops and seminars. They don't work. People don't have the time to visit someplace just to check out what's happening there. Even after a good turnout, the conversion rate is abysmal.

So what are people using nowadays? Nowadays, people are going for two main things. These are classified advertising and Google AdWords.

Classified Advertising

Direct advertising, or rather direct response advertising, is the best form of advertising that there is. In such an advertising technique, a direct response is solicited on an ad impression. This could be an email or an SMS. When people reply to these modes, they open up a route of communication with the advertiser.

The general route adopted here is:-
Ad impression → Direct response → Lead capture → Building the relationship → Pitching the right offer → Following up or closing the sale.

But again, the conversion rate is low, because you might have to send these advertisements to a lot of people in order to get a handful of responses.

Google AdWords

This is one of the most popular prospecting methods that is used by network marketing denizens nowadays. Its effect is considerable because you can directly reach your targeted clientele in this manner.

Chapter 8:

What It Takes to Be a Leader

Summary

Your network looks upon you with hope. You are their leader.

What It Takes to Be a Leader

You have to hone your personality to be a leader if you want to survive in the network marketing world. If you aren't the first in the race, people aren't going to remember you at all, because no one talks about the also-rans.

That is the reason you need to approach your network marketing strategies with a bit of caution. If you don't come across as a leader, you run the risk of being nothing more than a mere seller of goods.

One of the best ways to come across as a leader is to strike right at where the need is. People who sell usually speak about their products, their features, etc. But this is definitely the wrong approach. Instead of speaking about the product, you must speak about how the product can satisfy the requirement of the user.

This is a great quote in this respect:-

Nobody who bought a drill actually wanted a drill. They wanted a hole. Therefore, if you want to sell drills, you should advertise information about making holes; not information about drills.

- Perry Marshall

Be knowledgeable and pander right to the basest instinct of the customer when it comes to their requirement. That's the way to make them understand you know what it takes.

Here are some tips on how you can achieve this:-
- → Be natural, don't be imposing.
- → Be cool and casual with everyone, don't be too pushy. If you are, you come across as desperate and that's definitely not the trait of a successful leader.
- → Teach your market how to use the product and how it can satisfy their needs. When people see that a product is going to be useful for them, they will buy it from you and regard you as the leader in this domain.
- → Be innovative and dynamic. Take your methods online; that's where the 21st century marketing lies.

→ Keep learning.

→ Use highbrow prospecting tools. If people see that you have prospected them in a new-fangled manner, they are going to be more respectful to you and your business.

→ Always dress like a leader.

Chapter 9:

Interesting New-Age Products

Summary

Here are some products that are becoming useful in the current scenario.

Interesting New-Age Products

As long as you're offering cheap info products anyway, you might as well include a few products that will make you a little more money on the back end. You can't acquire the resell rights to everything, but you can often become an affiliate, which means you'll have the right to display links on your front-end page just as if the items were part of your store. Your visitors will just be taken elsewhere to finish the transaction—and you'll make a commission. Just make sure it automatically opens into a new window or tab rather than taking the visitor out of your page completely, or you lose out.

Three products are worth your attention. The Renegade Network Marketer, for example, will help train your future business partners how to go after their target market, which is exactly what you've been doing all along. That's definitely a skill you want your downline to have. Click on "Affiliates" to make sure you make your commission on the sale.

Another good product is Magnetic Sponsoring. These videos can help your downline supercharge their work.

Listen, you don't want to waste your time or anybody else's, so the possibilities inherent in providing these sorts of affiliate products is endless. You can literally make money on a pre-training program before anyone ever clogs up your downline. You'll avoid dead downline members who don't do anything except weigh your organization down, and you'll still make money whether they get serious or not. What could be better?

You can look to find as many of these products as you like, but try to make sure you read or use them before you go recommending them. After all you're basically putting your name and reputation on the line here. If the products aren't any good you're not doing yourself any favors by putting them up. Of course, you're not an affiliate marketer so you don't want to go too crazy. You want business partners, not people pingponging all over the Internet to read about being your business partner. Try to obtain a happy medium.

Chapter 10:

Parting Thoughts

Summary

Winding it up. A summary of everything in the eBook.

Parting Thoughts

Network marketing is no less challenging in the 21st century than it was before, but the best part is that now you have tools at your disposal that can help you do things in a better way. It is highly important that you use these new tools and evolve, or otherwise you will stay stuck in the rut and go nowhere.

It is highly important that you use the right prospecting methods. If you aren't able to do that, you might just fizzle out. Remember that people out there are using highly sophisticated new techniques even as we speak. Hence, it is important for you to stay one step ahead of them.

In closing, here are some of the things that you need to keep in mind when you are in a network marketing business that's geared for the 21st century.

→ Make sure you are always abreast of all the changes that are happening around you. You don't want to be caught with inadequate knowledge, which could wipe you out and make your competitors succeed.

→ Make the right decisions. This starts right from the time you choose your company. Select the right company – one that you are comfortable with and one whose compensation plans you understand fully.

→ Another thing you have to ascertain is that you are with the right people. Both your uplines and downlines are instrumental in your own success. The upline guides you and the downline takes you forward. Selecting a company with a good reputation is often an indicator that the people there are good, but it may not be a confirming factor.

→ Learn about the various compensation plans that exist. Contrary to what you think, these compensation plans are what can make you rich or keep you away from becoming that. Don't opt for front-loading companies.

→ Educate yourself on new prospecting techniques. Use all the resources of the Internet. The prospects of today like that.

→ Evolve yourself into a leader. Enroll yourself into personality development programs if needed. Learn what the customers really require of you and give them just that.

Conclusion

This was the new wave of network marketing, something that is much needed if you want to achieve any semblance of success today.

Use these techniques and see your venture soar.

All the Best to You!!!

www.ingramcontent.com/pod-product-compliance
Lightning Source LLC
Chambersburg PA
CBHW070904070326
40690CB00009B/1990